Kisses
FROM MOMMA

Shirley Thomas

ISBN 979-8-88851-215-9 (Paperback)
ISBN 979-8-88851-216-6 (Digital)

Copyright © 2023 Shirley Thomas
All rights reserved
First Edition

All rights reserved. No part of this publication may be reproduced, distributed, or transmitted in any form or by any means, including photocopying, recording, or other electronic or mechanical methods without the prior written permission of the publisher. For permission requests, solicit the publisher via the address below.

Covenant Books
11661 Hwy 707
Murrells Inlet, SC 29576
www.covenantbooks.com

CONTENTS

Letter 1:	In a Matter of Minutes	1
Letter 2:	One Call	4
Letter 3:	Shell-Shocked	6
Letter 4:	Deferred Hope	9
Letter 5:	Heartbreak Times Two	12
Letter 6:	Friends in All the Right Places	15
Letter 7:	When Practical Becomes Impractical	18
Letter 8:	There Is No Separation	21
Letter 9:	The Funeral	23
Letter 10:	Cherished Conversations	27
Letter 11:	Time Stops for No One	29
Letter 12:	When You Don't Know Your Words Are the Last Words	31
Letter 13:	Unanswered Questions	34
Letter 14:	When I Am Weak, God Is Strong	37
Letter 15:	A Deciding Moment	40
Letter 16:	The Mind Games	43
Letter 17:	Morning's Dawn	46
Letter 18:	A Vision Times Two	49
Letter 19:	Searching for Closure	52
Letter 20:	Forever Changed	55
Letter 21:	Endless Tears	58
Letter 22:	Signs from Heaven	60
Letter 23:	The Results Are In	63
Letter 24:	Overcoming Regrets and Guilt	66
Letter 25:	The Mind versus the Heart	69
Letter 26:	Learning to Forgive	71
Letter 27:	The First of Many	74

Letter 28: Limited Visitation 77
Letter 29: Your Family 79
Letter 30: Kisses from Momma 81

Epilogue...83

LETTER 1

In a Matter of Minutes

*Whereas ye know not what [shall be] on the morrow.
For what [is] your life? It is even a vapor, that appeared
for a little time, and then vanisheth away.*
—James 4:14

Dear Toby,

My mind was captured between two worlds: the one of reality, and the one of denial. The time was 3 a.m., and a part of me could not wait for daylight, while the other part did not want to see the sun come over the horizon. I was so tired of the darkness and the quietness of it; my thoughts seemed to vibrate inside, so I wanted the light of day. I wanted activity, but I knew in my heart that when the light would come, my half-dream-half-wish that my sweet son was alive would crumble. The light would spread the news of your death, which in turn would bring calls and visits to our home from people who loved and knew you. The light of day would mean life truly was going to go on without you. I wasn't ready for that—I would never be ready for it, but I knew the darkness could not stay. Time would not stand still and neither would the world. The reality of a life without you in it was slowly taking the center stage, all the while the reality of our former life of only hours ago was slipping away. And there I stood caught in the middle, wanting desperately to stay in the safe one yet being transported against my will into the one that had no stability.

How is it possible for my life to be forever changed in such a short space of time? My future and the future of my family were shattered into a billion pieces that would never on this side of heaven resemble any of my hopes and dreams. In one second, our lives completely changed. Our lives were far from perfect, but it had a frame that I recognized and claimed as our family. Now the frame was broken, and I knew in my heart it would never be the same again. One of us was missing and would not return. There was no amount of superglue to put us back together again. And there was absolutely nothing I could do about it!

Our lives changed right before midnight when we received *the* call. You know the one that no parent ever expects to receive, the call that has the power to take your breath away—yes, that's the one. No parent is ever ready for it; there's nothing in life that can prepare you. Yet it continues to happen, and it happened to us. In one second, our lives went from very comfortably normal to unbearably abnormal. The definition of *normal* is usual or ordinary, not strange, and mentally and physically healthy. That January morning began as an ordinary day and ended as far from normal as one can imagine. There are many ranges of normal when you compare families as well as many abnormal. What I was experiencing was off the charts of abnormal because no mother can imagine the deepest wound possible taking them to places they never knew existed. I now found myself in an unfamiliar place that seemed to have no end of pain.

It was a normal Saturday morning full of the usual routine chores and weekend plans. Your younger brother had a high school basketball game in a neighboring county, which we were planning to attend. There were clothes to laundry and a house to clean as well as church services the following day to prepare for. It was just a typical Saturday. I was hoping to possibly run into you and your two siblings and your families. It was hard to imagine the three of you being married and your younger brother Josh being the only one still living at home. Our blended family of three sons and one daughter had brought much joy to your daddy and me. There had been some heartache, but the joy far outweighed that aspect. But that one second brought so many emotions, so many questions, and so much pain that I hit the bottom of my joy resources. At the time, I didn't think I would ever find that joy again.

In one second on a normal day, a horrifying and overwhelming event invaded our lives. It was an uninvited intrusion. And there was absolutely nothing we could do to change or stop it. The motions were already in place. I felt like a bystander, just watching my life and the lives of my husband and children become a series of head-on crashes. I was totally powerless to do anything but watch. Inside I was screaming, "No, no!" but death had come and stolen someone precious from us despite my love, despite my faith, and despite my prayers. Why?

Our sweet Toby with the smile that made everything better was gone from this earth. No one would ever hear your laugh or see your eyes light up with mischief. No more hugs, no more "I love you" echoing in my ears. In one brief second that would forever be etched in my heart, you had vanished away.

Kisses from Momma

LETTER 2

One Call

Lo, I am with you always, even unto the end of the world.
—Matthew 28:20b

Dear son,

No one enjoys receiving a phone call late at night, especially if you're already asleep. The one received on the night of January 18 was the *one* no parent ever expects to receive. It's the call that changes lives forever. It's the call that you hope with all hope that it's a wrong number. It's the call that never ends in your mind; it replays over and over with the same outcome.

We returned home from your brother's basketball game around 9:30 p.m. and retired to bed around 10:30 p.m. It was a Saturday, and we had church services the next morning. I remember hearing the telephone ring and figuring it was a wrong number. I answered and could barely make out any words from the caller.

It took a few seconds to recognize your sister, Amye's, voice. She was sobbing, and the only words I could understand were, "He's not breathing." Everything else just ran together.

I kept repeating, "Who's not breathing, and where are you?"

After several minutes into the conversation, I realized she was talking about you. She was crying so hard, and I kept telling her to calm down and that everything would be okay. Because at that moment, I truly believed everything would be okay. I could not allow my mind or heart to believe anything other than that.

After verifying with her that the EMTs had been called and were on their way and that your beautiful wife, Brandi, was with her, and we continued our conversation about what had happened.

She told me Brandi had come home to find you on the couch. After not being able to wake you, she'd called Amye and the EMTs. Amye had performed CPR yet had been unsuccessful. I briefly spoke to Brandi, who was just as distraught as your sister. Her parents had been called as well.

By this time your younger brother, Josh, and your daddy were both awake and putting on their clothes, as I was, while still talking with them on the phone. The call couldn't have lasted more than a few minutes, yet in my mind, it is forever stuck on replay. There are times in my life when I can hear the conversation, and it seems to last forever. I can still hear the despair in their voices, and their heart-wrenching sobs. And I can still hear the calmness in my voice and feel that same determination in my heart that everything was going to be okay. Except it wasn't.

My only explanation of the strength and calmness I felt during that call was the strength of the Lord already saturating me for what was about to unfold in our lives. He was right there with me. He became and remains to this day my strength, my hope, and my shield. The shield that continually keeps my heart from completely shattering. I am forever thankful for His continuous presence. Without Him, I would not have made it through that one call, which had the power to change our lives forever. In the late hours of one day and the wee hours of the following day, I traveled to the end of the world in my mind—the end of a world with you in it to a world that you were no longer a part. Only through God was I able to make that horrible trip and remain whole. I alone was a broken mess, yet with the God of all Gods, I was whole.

Kisses from Momma

LETTER 3

Shell-Shocked

When thou passest through the waters, I will be with thee: and through the rivers they shall not overflow thee: when thou walkest through the fire, thou shalt not be burned; neither shall the flame kindle upon thee.
—Isaiah 43:2

> Definition of *shellshocked*—stunned, distressed, or exhausted from a prolonged trauma or an unexpected difficulty.

Dear Toby,

The night/early morning you left this earth is forever engraved in my mind. There was a progression of hope which burned brightly inside me, but it seemed to be quickly escaping as we waited for answers. I desperately wanted to hold on to a fragment of hope; I had to hold on to it. I couldn't and wouldn't allow my mind to think of the alternative for more than a few minutes, yet in my mind, it is forever stuck on replay. There are times in life when I can hear the conversation, and it seems to last forever. I can still hear the despair in their voices and their heart-wrenching sobs. And I can still hear the calmness in my voice and feel that same determination in my heart that everything was going to be okay.

The drive to the hospital was short because thankfully we lived only a few minutes away. Everyone, including Brandi's family (our extended family), reached the hospital at about the same time. We called your older brother Cahn right after our conversation with your sister. And there we were, the family who loved you, the family who were praying you were okay, the family who never saw or imagined the events we now found ourselves living. There we were. There was no escape, no rewind, no pause. We had to live every moment and every emotion not because we chose or wanted to but because there was no other choice.

We immediately inquired to see if we could go back and be with you and were told you had not arrived at the hospital yet. They were still working on you at your house. So you see, my son, to me that meant hope was still very much alive. We all found a seat in the almost-empty waiting area of the ER. The chairs were turquoise. The same chairs, or at least the same color of chairs, remain in the ER. Even now, if I go in or through the emergency room, the chairs always seem to stand out, and I instantly recall that night and all the emotions that were experienced in that room. It is one of those trigger points I must be mindful of and quickly escape from with the help of God.

We sat and we waited. No one spoke. I remember looking around and seeing these people who I love and know, yet they were almost unrecognizable that night. There was a look on each face—a look of desperation, a look of utter shock and unbelief, a look of extreme fear, and I knew my face mirrored the same expression or should I say lack of expression. Every passing second that we didn't hear anything, I could feel the hope in my heart retreating further and further away.

I'm not sure how many times I looked at the large clock in the waiting area. It seemed as if time had stopped in one sense, but in another, it seemed like it was rushing right on by. I felt like I'd become trapped in a time frame that I so desperately wanted to escape. My mind kept saying, *If you could just go back to a few hours ago, maybe things would be different.* If I could just wake up from this frozen dream... so many *if's*, *what's*, and *whys* captured my mind.

And I could tell by the expressions of all the folks waiting with me, their thoughts were echoing mine.

Each of us was silently praying. I could feel His presence as the waters of hopelessness kept getting higher and higher. I knew He was hearing, but I wanted action. I wanted God to change this situation. I *needed* God to change this situation.

As we continued to wait, I looked at the faces around me, and they all looked vacant. The only words to describe what I saw and sensed are shellshocked. We looked like we felt: we were trying to survive something none of us understood, something that was bigger than all of us combined. Our hearts were filled with an aching that can't be defined; our emotions were so raw that they physically and mentally hurt. And yet down somewhere deep, each of us was desperately clinging to a lifejacket of hope. But that hope was fading as every second passed, and our faces became more and more vacant. I believe the silent sobs that were ripping our hearts apart were more violent than the audible ones who cried out in great distress.

Every time the ER doors opened, we looked up, hoping to see someone come out and tell us you were okay, yet no one did. I needed to see you, to touch you; I needed to know you were breathing and were going to be okay.

We continued to wait with a ray of hope, but that ray was quickly becoming buried beneath the unknown.

Kisses from Momma

LETTER 4

Deferred Hope

> *Hope deferred maketh the heart sick: but when the desire cometh, it is a tree of life.*
> —Proverbs 13:12

Dearest Toby,

I'm not sure how long we continued to wait. Time seemed to stop during those hours. Friends, hearing something had happened, began to come by the hospital. We had no answers, and none of us were up for a small talk, so the visits were short. Some waited with us, and others left.

Finally, the doors leading to the emergency area opened, and a nurse came toward us. I think all of us stood up at the same time. I tried to read her face, which was without any expression. We were told to follow her. By this time, my hope had taken a severe beating, but just a sliver remained, hoping and praying that I was on my way to see you alive and well.

That sliver of hope was dashed quickly as I realized we were being led to a room off to the side. At that moment, my heart and my head began an inward argument. Being a volunteer chaplain, I knew what this room represented. This was the room family members were sent to when a patient was on the brink of death or had been pronounced dead in the ER. It was so still, so quiet. My body didn't want to enter the room. My mind wanted to hit replay and have a different story. Everything in me resisted what I knew was about to happen. We were told to take a seat as we crowded in the room, and someone would be in to speak with us soon.

I felt numb. My heart was racing, and it was difficult to breathe. Again, I felt a twist of emotions, wanting someone to come in quickly and say whatever they had to say and wanting them not to come in because I knew in my heart, I did not want to hear the words which were about to completely sever the shred of hope still desperately fighting to stay alive.

My sweet son, your mother's heart had been holding on for a miracle, and now I knew my needed miracle was not going to happen. I began to quiver inside. The disappearance of hope is an excruciating and painful event.

Shortly our local coroner entered the room. That was the moment when my hope of a miracle, my hope of a recovery, completely vanished. I wanted to run from the room. I wanted to grab your daddy and your siblings to protect them from the words that were about to change our lives forever. But there was nothing I could do to protect them or myself.

The coroner was struggling to speak, and there were tears in his eyes. Not only had he had to deliver devastating news many times, but he himself had experienced the pain and tragedy of losing a son to death, so he truly knew what we were experiencing. To this day, I continue to appreciate his genuine compassion that early January morning. No one can truly soften the devasting words that your loved one has died, but he did it with a heart of compassion.

As the words were spoken out loud, my heart and my mind rebelled inwardly. I didn't verbalize any of it, but inside everything was screaming, "No, no!" I could hear sobbing, I could see the faces, and I wanted to make it better for everyone, but I was powerless.

I don't remember leaving the room. I don't remember leaving the hospital. The next thing I remember is being in the car. Hours earlier hope had lived in my heart. Now there was a deep and vast hole in my heart. You were gone! Your body had been sent to the crime lab due to you being only twenty-six years old and having no known health issues. I had not been able to see you or say goodbye.

Somewhere deep down in my heart and mind, I knew you were now with Jesus, and I knew that should stir my hope again, but I must be honest, my son, at that moment I was very selfish. I wanted you with me and your family. I wanted to see the sparkle in your eyes. I wanted to hear your laugh. I wanted to watch you become a father one day. I wanted you! My hope was deferred for the moment, and my heart was so very sick.

We made the short drive home. Josh or your daddy didn't say anything and neither did I. There were no words to express what we were feeling. Our hopes and dreams for your life vanished; all the years that we would remain on earth had been altered, and there was no reversible action to be taken. We weren't going to be given a redo. How were we going to live without you?

I think I went on autopilot at this point. My physical body went through the motions, and my mind began to think about everything we now must do, but my heart was crushed. All I knew to do was ask the Lord to help me. It seemed every few seconds, inwardly, I was saying, "Please help me, Lord." And He did. Looking back now, I can see how the Lord upheld me when I didn't have the natural strength to do it myself. My family needed me, and while in myself, I felt like I had nothing to give, yet because of the power and love of God, I was able to survive the most difficult and devastating time of my life.

When everything around us is spiraling out of a control, we have a God who is completely in control and prepared and able to sustain us. My heart is full of gratitude and even amazement at the faithfulness of God. If not for Him, I do not know where I'd be today.

Kisses from Momma

LETTER 5

Heartbreak Times Two

> The Lord is nigh unto them that are of a broken heart; and saveth such as be of a contrite spirit. Many are the afflictions of the righteous: but the Lord delivereth him out of them all.
> —Psalm 34:18–19

Dear sweet son,

Our minds are so complicated. In those early hours of January 19, my thoughts were so scattered, yet because I'm an organized person for the most part, my mind was trying to organize everything that must be done. On top of the list was to inform your grandmother, lovingly known to you grandchildren as MaMa. This was something I'd never imagined having to do. I did not want to do it, but I didn't want to take the risk of someone else telling her. I waited until 5:30 a.m., and then your sister, younger brother, and I made the short trip to her house.

    The drive over to her home was quiet. I was rehearsing in my mind how to tell this woman who adored her grandchildren. How do you relay that kind of information to anyone, much less someone who you want to protect? I knew I had to tell her the truth, at least all we knew at the time, which was you were physically dead, and no one knew why. My mind and certainly my heart had not fully grasped the events of the last few six hours. I didn't know if I would ever fully comprehend what had happened.

Your grandmother quickly answered our light tap on the kitchen door. How many times had you gone barreling through those doors alongside your siblings? How many times had you raided her refrigerator, or she'd made scrambled eggs with cheese that each of you loved? How many times had her arms reached to hug you as you rushed through that door? That wouldn't happen again for you. I knew I was about to crush her heart. Her world was about to tumble down right beside mine.

She knew immediately something was wrong. We didn't usually stop by at five thirty in the morning, and I can't imagine what the three of us looked like as we stood there. There had been so many tears, I had become numb to them running down my face. Josh and Amye were trying to be strong for me and their grandmother, but they seemed to melt when she quickly asked what was wrong.

We made our way to the living room. She sat down in her beloved rocker-recliner, and I pulled a foot stool in front of her and sat down. Amye and Josh sat close by, and my brother came out of his bedroom to see what was going on. There's no easy way to break this kind of news, so I just dived right into the conversation. Tears ran down my face, and my voice was barely above a whisper as MaMa leaned in to hear my broken words. All the rehearsed words went down the drain as the words took on life as they came out of my mouth. I felt like it was someone else speaking.

Unbelief covered her face as she tried to comprehend what I was saying. I held her hands in mine, the same hands that had wiped tears from your face as you grew from an infant to toddler, to young adult, the same hands that held your hands as you learned to walk, the same hands that had held your hands only a few months earlier at your wedding. Those same hands reached out to wipe the tears from my face as the words came forth.

She had questions; your uncle had questions. We had few answers, which we shared. There was a range of emotions in that house that January morning, and none of them were familiar. Losing your grandfather, PaPa, eight years earlier had been difficult, and almost impossible for us, especially MaMa, but we had rallied around each other and survived it. I wasn't sure at that moment if we would survive losing you. But there was an inner knowing that we weren't doing this by ourselves. I knew even amid all the brokenness and pain, my Lord was near us. I knew my deliverer was working on my behalf and on my family's behalf. Because I had just finished doing something that only a few hours earlier I could not have thought possible to do. So even at that moment when I didn't feel anything like a survivor, I knew my God would make me more than a survivor; in time, He would make me an overcomer, if I would let Him.

The song "How Do You Mend a Broken Heart?" kept coming to my mind that morning as we sat with your MaMa and uncle. I decided there is only one answer, "You don't. Only God can mend it, and we would have to allow Him to mercifully and tenderly put the pieces back together again." I knew when He finished, it would look and feel differently than before, but that He would somehow put us all back together again. Through the years, I've learned the devastating, breathtaking pain subsides, but there's always a lingering knowing, a permanent scar that must be delicately retouched again and again by the hand of the Master.

Psalm 34:18 says, "the Lord is near to those of a broken heart." His Word is true. At every difficult, almost impossible task, during every conversation, every time a tear would fall, He was present. His Holy Spirit hovered all around me and was alive inside me. Without the assurance that He was with me, I would not have been able to handle the events which had suddenly turned my world upside down. I couldn't fix or change this terrible wrong; I could only choose to believe I would survive.

Kisses from Momma

LETTER 6

Friends in All the Right Places

God is our refuge and strength, a very present help in trouble. Therefore, we will not fear, though the earth be removed, and though the mountains be carried into the midst of the sea; the waters thereof roar and be troubled the mountains shake with the swelling thereof. Selah.

—Psalm 46:1–3

Dearest Toby,

These scriptures became alive for me over the next days, weeks, and months. I was in trouble, my earth had been shaken, and at times, I felt like I'd been dropped off into an unknown place that I would never return from again. The waters around me were troubled, and the mountains were shaking. Everything that had been firm, secure, and stable was now shaken. Yet I knew the One True King, Jesus Christ had not moved. His Word remained steadfast and true, and none of this had caught Him unaware. He became my refuge, my strength, and a very present help in my trouble. He calmed me, and He loved me during the worst of circumstances. His beautiful and amazing grace and mercy surrounded me. His peace penetrated my mind and heart. There were times I would question how I was even functioning—taking care of funeral arrangements, talking with family and friends—and then I would feel the presence of sweet

Jesus, and know that He had me in the palm of His hand, and He was breathing breaths of strength into me. How? I can't explain, but I knew it then, and I know it today because He continues to infuse me with His strength. He has become my dearest friend.

In those first few hours, I went into active mode. At two in the morning, I cleaned the house, cleaned the refrigerator, and tried to think about funeral arrangements. I wanted to be able to help your sweet wife in any way I could because I knew she was devastated by the events of the last hours.

God sent help to us through our church family. Within a few hours of us returning home, they arrived armed with food and coffee and most of all their love and compassion. They handled the calls, the visitors, and any and everything they could. Their sacrifice of love and time was such a gift to us. They stocked our refrigerator, and our neighbors, friends, coworkers, and so many folks who knew you brought food and supplies and offered their condolences. There was such an outpouring of love and concern. We have never forgotten all the calls and visits. Many of your heartbroken friends shared stories of the times they'd spent with you. Many of them brought laughter, and all of them brought tears. It was hard talking about you in the past tense while you were very much present within my heart. And you always will be *present* in my heart and mind.

During this first day of the new chapter of life without you, we had to begin making funeral arrangements. The necessary evils of death require families to force themselves to enter a thought pattern no one wants to travel, but there's no other choice, and with the help of our faithful God, we began to take the difficult steps. Your beautiful new bride was so heartbroken, but she wanted to be sure the services honored the prince charming of her life. She was not going to get the happily ever after she had envisioned, but she wanted your send-off to be special. During our conversations about your funeral, it was surreal. I found myself wanting to call you and ask your opinion. I also felt like we were discussing someone else's funeral. My mind could not completely wrap around the idea that this was you and your funeral.

Supernaturally, God was able to give our minds a break from the pain and shock so we could plan the service. Thankfully our funeral director was a lifetime friend of ours, plus one of his sons was a close friend of yours. Their compassion and kindness reached out to us, and that was priceless. Their experience guided us in many of our choices, and we are forever grateful for their invaluable help during this time. God was constantly present. Even when we had to painfully select a casket, I could feel the power of God strengthening me. No parent should ever have to make this decision, yet there we stood in a room full of caskets. It literally took my breath away. But step by step, we made the choices that had to be made. We could only hope we did you proud my son.

We are eternally grateful for the help God provided through the many friends that ministered to us through these first days and weeks. They always seemed to be present when we needed them the most. We were surrounded by their love and compassion, and without them, it would have been so much more difficult. And what they couldn't do, our God did! He undergirded me constantly with peace that gave me confidence that I and my family could survive this tragedy. I held on to my hope in Christ, that though I didn't see victory or feel victorious, eventually I would. It was a promise from God, and I had to choose to believe it!

Kisses from Momma

LETTER 7

When Practical Becomes Impractical

While we look not at the things which are seen, but at the things which are not seen: for the things which are seen are temporal; but the things which are not seen are eternal.
—2 Corinthians 4:18

The sun finally made its appearance after the longest night in history to me. We talked with Brandi again about the arrangements, and she gracefully agreed for us to choose the clothes for your burial. Shopping for you and your siblings had always been such a joy for me. Thoughts that this would be the last time I would have that privilege took my breath away, but I truly wanted to do it. We had a limited amount of time to get the task completed, but I knew we could do it. Buying clothes for you should have been a practical task, an enjoyable one, but in this case, buying clothes for your funeral viewing was as impractical as you can get. It was another one of those mixed-emotion events. There had been so many in the last twenty-four hours. I felt like I was on a roller-coaster ride that never stopped. I wanted off the ride, but no one could stop it.

You have always liked being stylishly dressed, even from a young boy. And you wore clothes well, especially formal attire. Everyone saw that at your recent wedding. I'd known it since prom days when you wore a tux and looked so handsome. So we wanted you to have a new suit, shirt, and tie, and that meant a trip to our then local men's shop.

When our minds are in crisis, they function in a completely different and irrational mode. It was extremely important to me that you look your very best for the viewing. It wasn't to impress anyone, except you, and I know that sounds crazy, and to be honest, I may have been reacting a little crazy at the time. There was a double-working of the mind going on within me. One part of me was trying to rationalize you were now present in heaven, and nothing we could do here on earth was going to compare with what you were experiencing, and the other part was crying out inside to do this one last thing for you. By putting a stylish suit on you, I would be doing the last earthly thing I could do, and I wanted to do it right. I wanted to please you one last time.

Living in a small town has a lot of perks, one being we knew the owners of the men's shop. So we arranged to meet with them early that Monday morning before they opened for business. I will be forever grateful to the beautiful young woman and co-owner who helped us make our selection. She demonstrated both compassion and professionalism as we looked through the dozens of suits searching for the right one. Then we found a tie and a shirt to match, and for a brief time, I felt like I had accomplished something important for you. Then reality crept back in, and this terrible outbreak of horror tried to lasso my heart—no matter how I tried to reason it out, the truth was we were preparing you to be buried!

We then took the purchased clothes and other needed items to the funeral home. This too was another blow to my emotions. Handing those clothes over to the funeral director, who personally greeted us, felt like I was betraying you like I was okay with everything. And I was so far from okay. Everything was happening too fast or too slowly. The measurement of time depended on what decision we were having to make. The funeral service was the next day, which at times seemed an eternity away, and then in my next thought, it seemed like it was quickly arriving, and I was not ready to say our final goodbyes.

Nothing can prepare a parent for the agony of planning a funeral service for their child. I wanted to claim my son, my Toby, yet physical death had robbed me of any earthly right to you. I wanted to fight what had happened. I wanted to wake up from the nightmare we were all living in. I wanted you to be alive. But there was absolutely nothing I could do except continue going forward. My husband and my other children and grandchildren needed me. I still had a purpose, and at this point, walking out of that funeral home, I made up my mind I was going to push myself with God's help to survive. I had to keep my focus on the things I could not see, the things that are eternal. Because of my faith in Jesus Christ and His Word, I knew this was only a temporary separation. We would be together again, never to be apart again. Physical death is only temporary, and if you're a believer, once physical death happens, then you are alive with Christ and become a full-time resident in heaven. I chose that day, and I have chosen every day since to believe that we will be together again for eternity.

Kisses from Momma

LETTER 8

There Is No Separation

For I am persuaded, that neither death, nor life, nor angels, nor principalities, nor powers, nor things present, nor things to come, nor height, nor depth, nor any other creature, shall be able to separate us from the love of God, which is in Christ Jesus our Lord.
—Romans 8:38–39

Dear son,

The southern tradition of viewing the body of a physically dead person is barbaric when you think about it. There's no life in those bodies, and in one sense, it's just a horrible reminder that the person you love is just a shell. The heart, the love, and the laughter are no longer present. I knew in my heart you were not in that body lying in the coffin we'd picked out the day before, but in the first few minutes of seeing the still body that had once housed your beautiful personality, my knees buckled, my lungs exploded, and I felt myself falling to the carpet. Your daddy and big brother Cahn caught me before I hit the floor. For a few seconds, everything went numb, and I couldn't hear. There was complete silence, yet I felt the presence of my Lord and Savior. It's difficult to explain, but I knew that in the middle of the worst day of my life, being separated from you, I was not separated from my Jesus. Even though I couldn't see Him, He was ever present. Your body was right before me; I could see you, but we were separated by the gulf of physical death. On the other hand, Jesus, who I could not see, was so present I could feel Him, and His uncompromising love surround me in that room.

After a few minutes, I stood again and looked at your body. Your eyes were closed, and your mouth, so often filled with laughter, was shut. The sparkle in your eyes would never be seen again, and the joy in your voice was silenced forever on this side of heaven. The Toby I had loved for over twenty-six years was not in that casket. My heart was searching for you, but I knew I would never find you again here on earth.

I quickly forced myself to recover and turn my focus on my family. Your beautiful bride was devastated. Only a few months earlier, the two of you had shared a fairy-tale wedding. Now the story had taken a dark and twisted turn, and there was no exit or return. My motherly instincts overruled my own grief, and I went to her as well as to your brothers and sister. Words were not necessary; in times like this, there's an unspoken language that prevails. Our tears spoke louder than any verbal words.

I'm not sure how long we stayed in the viewing room of the funeral home. It was another of the many events that seemed to be a mixture of too much time and not enough time. There was a part of me that didn't want to leave and another part that couldn't get out of the room fast enough. Since this was a private viewing for the family, and many of your friends were waiting, we decided to leave so others could have time with you (or should I say with your body).

As we were leaving, I realized that just as the love of God could not be separated from me as Romans 8:38–39 states neither could our love be separated. You were forever sealed in my heart, and even the physical separation we were now experiencing could not and would not ever separate our love. I loved you from the moment I knew I was pregnant, and I will always love you—forever and forever.

Kisses from Momma

LETTER 9

The Funeral

Good people pass away; the godly often die before their time.
But no one seems to care or wonder why.
No one seems to understand
that God is protecting them from the evil to come.
For those who follow godly paths
will rest in peace when they die.

—Isaiah 57:1–2 (NLT)

Dear son,

The days following your departure are a blur. Some events and thoughts stand out and will always be a part of me, while others are distorted and broken. I may remember pieces but not the whole part of a conversation or task. I do remember it was not a day I wanted to experience, and I remember the dream state I seemed to find myself in, yet I couldn't wake up from it.

    We visited the funeral home early that morning so we could say our final goodbyes in private. You have always been such a beautiful blessing in our lives, just as your sister and brothers are. I realized that morning as I memorized every part of your face, your fingers, your shoulders, and your hair that so much of your beauty and heart was inward, and it penetrated through your flesh body. Now that the real you was gone, the precious brightness was gone from the physical form my eyes lingered upon for one last time. Yet I wanted to stay in that moment forever. Death takes away so many of our choices because it is final on this earth. But I had hope that day, and I continue to have that same hope that we will be together again.

I don't remember what I wore; in fact, I don't remember anything about the pre-funeral morning. My first recollection of the day is being at the funeral home to say goodbye and then in the church. It was the beautiful little church where you and your bride were married just a few months previously. I remembered how handsome you looked standing there waiting to see the love of your life make her entrance. What a contrast now! How can it even be possible? These were the thoughts that took possession of my mind.

I remember thinking over and over, *A terrible mistake had been made. This could not be my son Toby!*

The day of your funeral certainly tested our faith, and at the time, I wondered if we would pass or not. Now years after, I can truthfully say, "We passed." But it was only through the strength of our God, who we depended on for every second of each day, especially the day of your funeral service.

The church was packed, plus there was a large crowd standing outside that January morning. Family, friends, coworkers of yours, and many people I didn't recognize at the time came to say goodbye to you and express their sympathy to us.

Brandi did an excellent job in planning your service. Our friend and pastor that we'd asked to speak did an excellent job. The songs Brandi selected were perfect. The floral arrangements that had been sent by people who loved you and us were beautiful. You would have loved them.

After the service, I remember the short walk from the church to the cemetery. It was so quiet. It seemed the world stood still for just a bit as we all gathered to say our final farewells. My heart was shattered, yet I wanted to remain strong for my family, especially your nephew Jordan. He worshipped you, and your sudden death was taking a toll on him. I asked him to sit with me at the gravesite. And he quickly got in my lap. I'm not sure who held on to whom the tightest, me or him. I can still hear the sobs coming from your sister and others around us. I remember the sorrow on the faces of people who loved you. I remember the longing in my heart to make things better for you siblings and the man who stood by my side and loved you since the day he came into our lives when you were only five years old. I remember silently praying to God to help them all because I knew I had nothing to give them at that time, except my love and prayers. I remember so much, yet there's so much I don't.

I reflect now on that day, and I see how strong each of us was trying to be for each other, down to sweet Jordan. Your physical death made a great impact on him, and even to this day, he will tear up sometimes when we reminisce. But we share much laughter as well when we recall some of your adventures.

That was a painful day. It was something no parent should ever endure, but we did. And so do many other parents. Every day somewhere, a parent is burying their child. Your life and the lives of others are being cut short. And we as parents are left to figure out how to live our lives every day, without our children. We can say it's not fair, but it happens.

The only thing that sustained me that day was Jesus Christ and His promises. Personally, I don't believe that Christians or any other human being receives their angel wings when they physically die. God already has His angels. I believe you walked right into heaven because of the crown of righteousness you received the day you accepted Jesus Christ as your Savior. I remember the day you accepted Jesus into your heart. You were only seven, and during the altar service, you raised your hand, and immediately you received the crown of righteousness. At twenty-six, you received the fullness of that crown. You graduated right out of earth school and transferred to living with Jesus because of the decision you made at seven years old. I know through the years between you had many struggles, failures, and successes, but you remained in contact with Jesus. I remember the talks we had about how you tried running from Jesus, but He always found you. I'm so glad the decision you made that Sunday night enabled me the day of that funeral and continues to enable me to have complete peace about your destiny after your physical death. I have the hope of Christ in my heart that keeps pushing me forward every day.

We got through that day because we had no other option. And I thanked God then and every day for His promise in 2 Timothy 4:8, "Henceforth there is laid up for me a crown of righteousness, which the Lord, the righteous judge, shall give me at that day: and not to me only, but unto them also that love His appearing."

Kisses from Momma

LETTER 10

Cherished Conversations

Who is a wise man and endued with knowledge among you? Let him show out of a good conversation his works with meekness of wisdom.
—James 13:10

Dear Toby,

I believe now is a good time to talk about some of our last conversations. There's so much I wished I had said, but I never dreamed I wouldn't have the opportunity to say over and over how much I loved you, what a blessing from God you were in our lives, and how extremely proud I was of all your accomplishments. I can only hope you knew.

    I am thankful however for the time we spent together right before your wedding. You would come over to talk about the wedding, and somehow, we would get sidetracked and just talk about life. I cherish every word that we shared. Thank you for choosing to spend that time with me. We were able to clear the air about a few delicate subjects and decisions you'd made through the later years, and most importantly, you assured me of your relationship with Jesus Christ. I know in my heart our footsteps were ordered by God for those divine appointments, and I am so thankful.

We talked about the good times, and the not-so-good times. We discussed the past, the present, and the future. I didn't know our future was going to be cut short.

You expressed concerns about being a good husband, and I remember telling you that you would be a great husband. It thrilled my heart when you talked about starting a family with Brandi in the future. You would have been an excellent daddy.

During one of our conversations, you mentioned how you'd been running from God but wanted to surrender completely. You assured me you were still a believer, who had messed up, but that you never severed your heart relationship with God and prayed every night. You mentioned how you talked to God all through the day about your problems, asking for His help, and truly wanting to please Him. My heart was so filled with thanksgiving that even though you had made some wrong choices (just like the rest of us), you kept the lines open to God.

You ask for my forgiveness for the times you'd disappointed me and the times you had created worry or stress with your choices. That was such a sweet moment as I hugged you with tears in my eyes. I loved you unconditionally, so regardless of the choices you made, whether good or bad, nothing was going to change my love for you then or now. But the sincerity of your words has certainly made the years after your transition to heaven much more tolerable as I envision our future in heaven together. I'm so thankful for these conversations.

We didn't get the fairy-tale ending we talked about, but I did receive an assurance that all was right between you and God, and we had the opportunity to clear the air over issues that had been under the surface for several years. And I knew we both understood the love we had for each other.

The slate was wiped clean through our conversations. We laughed, we cried, and we looked to the future. My heart was so full of love for you, and I was so excited to see you move into the next phase of your life. I didn't realize how short that phase here on earth would be.

Kisses from Momma

LETTER 11

Time Stops for No One

*The Lord is close to the brokenhearted and
saves those who are crushed in spirit.*
—Psalm 34:18

Dear Toby,

Those first few days were a game of survival for us. I can recall praying many times for God to help me survive—whatever the task was—I needed Him; I had to have Him. And He did not disappoint. Your physical death and our separation were a mountain that I didn't want to climb, yet there were continual reminders of it in my path. I searched for a quick exit, but there was none to be found.

Because of the faithfulness of a loving God, buried beneath the overwhelming sadness and grief was the ever-present peace of God. I chose to believe it was there by faith, not because I felt it at the time. His loving arms were a constant companion to me, even when I wasn't consciously aware of His amazing presence. He was there—all the time—and every footstep I made up that dark mountain was taken with Him carrying me.

One of the most difficult realizations came on our drive home from the funeral. We'd just gone through the most horrific event having our hearts ripped apart as we said our goodbyes to you. It felt like the whole world had stopped. But I soon realized that was not the case. Life continued all around me. People were coming and going. The banks and retail shops were open for business; the force of life had not ceased or even slowed down.

Their lives are normal. Mine will never be normal again. People have no clue how quickly things can change, were my thoughts as I silently observed people come and go on a normal day.

Life can be so unfair and cruel, I thought to myself.

I reflected on how only a few days ago I was one of those people, taking life for granted. Death doesn't wait on an invitation or permission; it sometimes sneaks into a family and steals pieces of our hearts.

I realize now I was envious of those seemingly normal people with normal lives. Their hearts were still intact. They had not attended a funeral, being forced to say goodbye to someone they loved and would never see again on this earth. Their hearts were not being shattered, piece by piece.

Because of that experience, when there's a death in our community, I began praying for the family and friends, whose lives, just like ours, will never be the same. And now I can thank God that life did continue for me and our beautiful family. Every day is filled with love and memories of you. The rubble of sadness and grief is not as towering today as it was on the day of your farewell service. There will always be a residue in my heart, but God has lessened the intense pain of it. We say the cliché that time heals all wounds. I'm not so sure about that, but I can honestly say, "My God has and continues to supernaturally heal all my wounds. I had to make the choice to allow Him to heal me, and He did. Though my spirit was crushed, and I was completely brokenhearted, He saved me then, and He continues to save me from the crashing waves of grief that could have completely overtaken me."

Kisses from Momma

LETTER 12

When You Don't Know Your Words Are the Last Words

> The steps of a good man are ordered by the
> Lord: and he delighteth in his way.
> —Psalm 37:23

Dear son,

The last time I saw you on this earth was not a prearranged meeting—it was simply an unexpected and random event of the two of us being at the same place at the same time. We had not planned to meet that day, but our God had other plans.

While it is so difficult for my mind to grasp the knowledge that your physical death a few days later was not a surprise to God and that He knows what every day looks like for each of us, I do believe with all my heart that He ordered our steps that evening.

After spending a long day with your uncle and MaMa in Warner Robins at doctors' offices, I had got them settled in at their home and had run to a fast-food restaurant to pick up supper for them. Another *chance* happening was we parked right by each other, arriving only a few seconds apart.

Neither of us realized this would be the last time we would see each other in person, speak to each other face to face, or reach out to give our final hugs on this earth. During the days, weeks, and months, and to be honest, even now, I was and continue to be so thankful for those minutes we shared. They will always be in my heart. I've discovered that physical death certainly separates us from each other, but it does not have the power to separate us from our memories. They are forever engraved in my heart and are always available for me to reflect upon and share with others.

I'm so thankful I serve a God who plans my every step every single day. He knows the beginning and the end of each of us and is always looking out for our good.

That Thursday, I fell into the steps God had already ordained for me to walk. It was not by chance or luck, it was by His grace and mercy that not only He ordered my steps that day but yours as well.

You looked tired that evening, but your beautiful eyes had that magical sparkle and that seemingly always-present smile on your face. Brandi as always looked amazing, and the two of you together looked like loving newlyweds, which was exactly what you were. You were working full-time and entering your final semester at school. You were scheduled to graduate in May at the top of your class. Your life seemed to be on track; you were happy and preparing for a great future.

As always, our conversation was one filled with laughter. After we received our to-go orders, we walked back to our vehicles. Hugs, kisses, and promises to get together soon were exchanged. You, being the gentleman you always were, opened my car door for me, leaned in, gave me that last kiss on the cheek, and said, "I love you, Momma," and I returned those powerful words to you.

I pulled out of the parking lot first, and you pulled out right behind me. I remember looking in my rearview mirror and seeing both of you waving and smiling. That single moment and those words are forever established in my memory and heart. That was the last time we saw each other on this earth. Those were the last words we spoke to each other on this earth—the last words and final glances of my beautiful son, who only a few days later would be forever gone from our presence.

I'm so thankful our last words were not of anger, frustration, or anything negative. There are no regrets on my end of anything that was said. My only regret is that we didn't linger a bit longer that January Thursday evening.

Words are powerful, and even though we didn't always agree, and through the years, there were many tests, we always maintained respect and love for each other as mother and son. We had serious conversations but never screaming matches, saying things that can never be erased. Knowing that our words were never filled with poisonous blame or bitterness brings great comfort to my heart now.

I learned a powerful lesson from that ordained day. Never allow harsh or angry words to be in your conversation with anyone, especially those you love with all your heart. Neither of us had any idea that would be our last conversation; most of the time we don't know. I've learned to forgive quickly and forget the negative things. Speak in love and remember the positive things. Regret can be such a destructive emotion and only adds to the pain and grief we experience after losing someone we love. Love conquers all! And I sure love you, son!

Kisses from Momma

LETTER 13

Unanswered Questions

Come unto me all that labor and are heavy-laden, and I will give you rest. Take my yoke upon you and learn of me; for I am meek and lowly in heart: and ye shall find rest unto your souls. For my yoke is easy and my burden is light.
—Matthew 11:28–30

Dear son,

Living in a small town means everybody knows everybody, or at least they know someone who knows someone who knows someone. And people speculate, and those speculations can turn into big-time gossip, having maybe a tiny fiber of truth to the situation but mostly just plain speculation and gossip.

Those first few days and weeks brought many of those stories to our ears. We did not know what had happened. We had not heard from the authorities because they didn't have any answers at the time. So there were many unanswered questions.

People unknowingly can be so cruel and invasive. People we'd not seen for years came to pay their "respects," and their curiosity always surfaced. While we appreciated their gestures of sympathy and concern, their questions about what happened and wanting to know private details really bothered me. I understand the curiosity, especially in a situation like we found ourselves, but I learned through our experience to never ask those questions. They are not necessary or helpful and do not bring comfort or change what has happened.

We understood though none of us liked it, that due to your young age and no known medical issues, an autopsy had to be performed and an investigation by our local law enforcement and GBI had to be conducted. They would have questions as well that at the time seemed so personal and intrusive, yet we cooperated with them. This was a first for our family, so it was unsettling, to say the least having to go to the GBI offices and be interrogated about our son. Our minds understood the necessity of it, but our hearts were still shattered and still dealing with the events which had so drastically changed our lives. Thankfully the officials who questioned us were as sympathetic and professional as they could be, but it still was very uncomfortable.

I remember one Christian lady and her husband coming by our home that first day after you left us. Her intentions were good, but the questions she asked were—number one—none of her business and very personal. Of course, I didn't have any answers for her, which prompted them to leave quickly. I learned a valuable lesson that day. Sure, the questions are there but never verbalized them to the family. If they know and want to share that's okay, but let it be their decision whether to discuss it.

There were many rumors floating around, but I chose not to take any of them to heart. Nothing official had been reported to us, and I knew how small-town thinking and gossip can be, so I turned a deaf ear to most of the rumors. People who have not experienced a tragic event such as the unexpected death of a family member cannot understand how painful the questions can be to that mother, daddy, sibling, or grandparent. And the bottom line is answers do not change anything. Many will comment, "Well, I know when you have the answers, you will have some closure and peace." But that's not true. Answers can bring more confusion and pain.

My only peace and closure were through Jesus Christ. I was heavy-laden with questions, grief, and all the other emotions that were constantly trying to camp out in my mind and heart. I needed rest from it, and thankfully, I knew where to go to find what I needed and had to have. It wasn't to the GBI office, it wasn't to these friends who thought they were being a comfort to me, and at the time, it wasn't to my family because they were in as much pain and grief as I was. I had to run to the only One who could give me peace and rest. And He was right there for me—every single time.

Kisses from Momma

LETTER 14

When I Am Weak, God Is Strong

Since ye seek a proof of Christ speaking in me, which to you-ward is not weak, but is mighty in you. For though He was crucified through weakness, yet He liveth by the power of God. For we also are weak in Him, but we shall live with Him by the power of God toward you.
—2 Corinthians 13:3–4

Dear Toby,

Those first few days after you left were very difficult for me. There was a large part of me who wanted to hide from anyone. That part of me didn't want to talk or see anyone, and I didn't want to answer any questions. I knew I didn't have any answers, plus I didn't feel like it was anyone's business. I know people are just naturally curious, but at the time, I felt it was an intrusion of our privacy. Some were well-meaning, others just nosy, but their insensitivity was a thorn in my side at the time. But it was a learning tool for me to practice when I minister to moms and families going through the same thing. The truth of the matter is what happened doesn't change the harsh reality that their daughter or son is not coming back no matter what happened. Sometimes, as in our case, we didn't know for weeks and had no answers, and in other cases, the families may not be comfortable talking about what happened. When they want to talk about it, they will, or they may never. Either way, my job is to give them hope and encouragement, not ask questions. This I learned from the experience of handling the overwhelming questions of what happened to you.

There was another part of me who wanted to see and talk to those who stopped by our home or called to let us know they loved us and were praying for us. So many of your friends from school and your workplace stopped by to see us, and others called. Their hearts were broken, and they couldn't believe you were gone. Many would share memories, bringing laughter and tears. Friends of your sister and brothers piled into the house, reminding me of the days our home was filled with young people all the time. But now the fun and carefree times which had filled our home were replaced with shock and grief. I received and gave many hugs those first couple of days.

All these folks loved you, they truly did, and their concern for us was overwhelming. Most of them didn't know what to say and neither did I. They just offered their hugs, their tears, and their sweet stories, and I in return offered my wounded heart to them. I am eternally thankful that the God of Abraham, Isaac, and Jacob is my God too because as I listened to each one as they shared their memories, their bewilderment, and their fears, the strength of my God rose in me. The Holy Spirit inside me was strong and faithful to have the correct response and to reach out in love to everyone who visited or called during those first few days. I don't remember our conversations, but I do remember their faces before our conversations and after. Because in my weakness, I allowed Him to be strong in me and reach out and touch these beautiful friends; they received ministry from the Great I Am. It was not me by any means; it was Him. I fell in love with Him more and more as I realized how truly He wants to be in our lives, especially in the darkest moments of our lives.

Surviving those first few days was nothing short of a miracle for me, and the miracle giver was Jesus Christ. He knew my weaknesses, and I discovered strength from Him that I never understood prior to this unexpected event in our lives. I am forever grateful for the power of His love, peace, and strength. He delivered me those days from darkness I could have easily wandered into permanently—darkness that wanted to consume and destroy me. But because he is strong when we are weak, I was able to remain in His light.

You were so loved, my son. The demonstration of the love and heartbreak by our community was truly overwhelming. And you are still missed by so many. You have not been nor will ever be forgotten.

Kisses from Momma

LETTER 15

A Deciding Moment

But we all, with open face beholding as in a glass the glory of the Lord, are changed into the same image from glory to glory, even as by the Spirit of the Lord.
—2 Corinthians 3:18

Dear Toby,

During the weeks and months following your physical death, there were many deciding moments in my life. Each time I had a choice; I could move on into a future without you, or I could get stuck in grief. One of the most significant moments included your nephew, Jordan.

Jordan was ten years old when you left this earth. He absolutely adored you and loved it when you spent time with him. His little heart was broken, and he couldn't understand why you had to leave. Neither could the rest of us, but we tried to put on a brave face. One thing I've discovered over the years, children usually can sense when adults are *acting*, and that's exactly what I was doing. Children recognize the real and the false, and I could see in Jordan's eyes that he knew I wasn't the same Grandmommy I'd been before your departure.

I remember that morning so vividly. Jordan was visiting me on a Saturday morning, and I was going through the motions when I saw him observing me. It seemed as if he was searching for his real grandmommy, the one with joy and peace, the fun grandmommy. I realized I had turned into someone he didn't recognize, and I immediately knew I had to stop the self-pity, get rid of the guilt, and figure out how to overcome the grief. I knew Who my answer was, but I realized I wasn't allowing God to help me. Somewhere through the process, I had begun to think these abnormal feelings I was experiencing were normal. Jordan had two images of me—the grandmommy before Toby's death and the one after his death. The images didn't match; in fact, they didn't even resemble.

And then I had an image of Jordan as a grown man (as he is today) and hearing him say, "Grandmommy was never the same after Toby went to heaven."

That image broke my heart and prompted me right then to pull him close and hug him, telling him how sorry I was. Of course, he didn't know that God had just done a miraculous *wake-up* call in my life. But I believe he did sense a change in me. I knew I had to change. I had so much to be thankful for—your amazing sister, your two awesome brothers, and at that time three beautiful grandchildren, plus the very best husband who loves me unconditionally. My life was so blessed; I had so many reasons to be joyful and grateful, yet I had been focusing only on my loss. Losing you had become the focal point in my life; it seemed that my every thought was consumed with missing you. Until that moment, I hadn't realized my life was a masquerade. I was pretending everything was okay, instead of realizing everything really was okay even though it didn't feel nor would ever feel okay. God had used a ten-year-old to speak into my life.

That Saturday morning, I made the decision that I would not allow my husband, children, or grandchildren to be robbed of the *me* God created me to be. And I didn't want to be robbed of the opportunities and the joy of being who He created me to be in this life. My desire was to fulfill the purpose and call on my life.

In making that decision, I realized it didn't lessen the call I had on being your momma, which is a lie the enemy had formed in my mind. Before that moment, I'd thought if I stopped focusing on you and your death, my role as your momma would fade. I understood then, and I know now that will never happen. I will always be your momma!

Kisses from Momma

LETTER 16

The Mind Games

They profess that they know God; but in works they deny Him, being abominable, and disobedient, and unto every good work reprobate.
—Titus 1:16

Dear Toby,

Titus 1:16 isn't an encouraging verse, is it? When grief becomes your lifestyle by default, not choice, it can lead you to that place described in the verse. I know because it could have easily become me. Death and grief are not very accommodating. Everything is thrown out of proportion when they hang around. Those affected by the two, sometimes find themselves going on autopilot. You do what you're supposed to do, you say what you're supposed to say, and you lose yourself to the facade of what you think you're supposed to look and act like. You put on that "I'm okay" face, and you hope that everyone around you is buying it.

Since I'm a reader, I searched for books to help me get out of the funk I found myself navigating through. At the time, there were few resources. I believe because of that, a dream was birthed in me to do this collection of letters as a book. My prayers and hopes are that it will help someone walking the path we've walked; somehow let them know that they're not alone and that they will not only survive but also overcome the devastation of losing a child to an early death.

I came to understand quickly that there's no right or wrong way to get through the steps of grief. Everyone goes through them at a different pace and reacts in a different manner. I also learned to be careful who I shared my feelings with because some who had no idea of what we as a family were experiencing would offer shallow advice and sometimes even judgmental words. I know they meant well, but their words would only take me back to the pit of grief that I'd been digging out of for weeks. But then there were those who'd walked the path, encouraged me, and let me know I wasn't losing my mind (which at times I was sure), and they prayed with me, hugged me, and gave me hope.

Autopilot puts you in a frozen emotional state. Turning off the autopilot was a decision I had to make and stick to regardless of how I felt. Autopilot meant walking around and wearing a fake smile yet feeling empty of any real joy. I remember hoping no one would say anything to me about you or your death because I knew how difficult it would be to keep my *happy* mask in place. Inside my heart was continually crying, while on the outside I tried to maintain a composed image. It was a daily battle, and most days I was not the winner.

Grief is a very real emotion, and it must be experienced for a season. It should not be a terminal way of living. I got tired of pretending; I'd never like phonies, and I discovered I didn't like being one either. Plus I knew the Great I Am, the One who knew me before I was conceived in my mother's womb. I no longer wanted to deny Him or His power in my life. I didn't want to continue being disobedient, abominable, or reprobate. I had to change!

This is a personal decision and can only be made by each individual. It's not something anyone can tell you to do, and *poof*, it just happens. It is a conscious choice and one I made and continue to make every day. I can only say Jesus died a painful death to purchase freedom from grief for me. He wants me to have life and have it more abundantly.

Autopilot was not a way of life for me. I experienced it, and I did not like it, so I asked God to be the captain of my journey, and I've never regretted it. Not only does He know what my future holds for me but He also loves me even when I wander off course, and He gently takes my hand and secures my steps through every part of my walk. Masks and false smiles are no longer necessary. Through Him, I can experience the joy of the Lord which becomes my strength, and I can experience it 24-7 every single day! And in the moments when grief would find its way in for a moment, He continues to hold my hand and gently lifts me out of the despairs and pitfalls of grief. I discovered I always have a choice. I can stay and become a resident of that gulf of grief, or I can occasionally visit and leave quickly. I chose to leave quickly. It doesn't mean I don't miss you every single day, my sweet Toby, but it does mean I no longer allow grief and sorrow to rule me. The One True God rules my mind. And I am so thankful!

Kisses from Momma

LETTER 17

Morning's Dawn

*For our light affliction, which is but for a moment,
worketh for us a far more exceeding and weight of glory:
while we look not at the things which are seen, but at the
things which are not seen: for the things which are seen are
temporal; but the things which are not seen are eternal.*
—2 Corinthians 4:17–18

Dear son,

The aftermath of your physical death continued. I've weathered so many sleepless nights. I have begun to dread the end of daylight. And I know from studying His Word that dread is a form of fear. And fear comes from the enemy. I understand the source of my fear of the night hours, and I know I must become victorious in this aspect of my lie. God created my body to need rest, and a good night's sleep is vital to that rest.

The only time I sleep was from pure exhaustion, and that was not a healthy rest. The quietness of the night allowed all the dark shadows to expand in my mind. So many nights I had gotten out of bed and searched God's Word for comfort and peace so my bombarded mind could rest. Sometimes it seemed to help, while other times I felt no relief. My spirit knows He is always helping me, comforting and counseling me because that's His job, yet there were so many times I didn't feel Him. I know my feelings do not make Him any less present in my life, but I desperately needed to feel Him. I miss you so much, and my heart physically hurts every night. There's a war going on and the enemy is doing his job well.

John 10:10 tells us the enemy came to steal, kill, and destroy. And he is using every evil tactic to overpower me, yet I have to remind myself of the other part of that verse—*but* Jesus came that I might I have life and have it more abundantly. I must choose one, and I want to choose *life, abundant life*! I began to read His Word every night first and not wait until the bad dreams would awaken me. My dreams remained the same 90 percent of the time. The same dream over and over. I would dream that everything that had happened in the previous months was just a dream. For a moment in my dream (or maybe nightmare), I would experience such excitement and peace because I would believe you were still alive. And then in the same dream, I would realize that was a misconception, and you were indeed gone forever from this earth, and then the devastating realization would shatter the excitement and peace I briefly experienced. It was a vicious cycle, and I couldn't seem to get out of it.

Even during the lack of sleep and rest, God sustained me, and I have been able to function both physically and mentally. It was by a supernatural means, and His name is Jesus.

Finally, I discovered this scripture, "When you lie down, you will not be afraid, when you lie down, your sleep will be sweet" (Proverbs 3:24). And every night I would repeat these Words over my sleep. Rest didn't come immediately, but I refused to give up, and I became diligent and used my mustard-seed-size faith to believe that sweet sleep was on its way, and it would find me. At first, I began sleeping four to five uninterrupted hours, a couple of times a week. Within six months, my sleep pattern was back to almost normal. Even now, my sweet son, there are still certain times of the year; those dreams will resurface, but my God's Word is truth; He will give me sweet sleep. All I must do is believe and receive.

Though your face is never far from me, I am no longer tormented by it at night. I believe what 2 Corinthians 4:17–18 tells me. Afterall what is a moment in God's time? God is not limited by time. Time has no value to Him, only to us. His timetable is not the same as mine, and I cannot put Him on mine. Do I consider your death a light affliction? In the natural, of course not, but supernaturally, looking to Him, the death of a loved one is a light affliction in the revelation of the vastness of God. How can I say that? Because I know with certainty the God of all creation has made an eternal promise that we will be together again, and that is the exceeding and eternal weight of glory I fasten myself to every day. No longer do I look at the things I see; I look to the things I cannot see, and these things are eternal. I live in a spiritual light that never dims.

Kisses from Momma!

LETTER 18

A Vision Times Two

And it shall come to pass afterward, that I will pour out my spirit upon all flesh; and your sons and your daughters shall prophesy, your old men shall dream dreams, your young men shall see visions.
—Joel 2:28

Dear Toby,

My sweet Toby! How I long to sit and talk with you face to face. My heart longs to hear your voice, and sometimes as I share my thoughts through these letters, I can almost hear you respond, and sometimes I hear your laughter. I miss you, but I know the days are short until we are together. I thank God every day for His glorious plan of redemption and eternal life.

I want to expound a bit more about my dreams. Not all of them have been bad; in fact, some of them have been a blessing. I know you will understand when I share this with you, even though others will not. Well, here goes!

Those previous dreams began to be less and less, and then I settled into occasionally dreaming about you. These dreams were filled with a *feeling* of being with you. They didn't bring confusion or fear but rather a feeling of peace and contentment. I knew they were dreams, yet they felt so real. Now years later, I can't say I truly remember what most of the dreams were about. I just remember the beautiful feeling of peace they brought to my weary mind.

However, there's one dream, or what I call a vision, which I will never forget. Many might not understand or even believe what I'm going to share, but I know it happened, and I know it was real.

This dream or vision happened a few months after your departure. I remember praying, and as I'd learned to do from the weeks of dreams full of sadness and tears, I asked God for a peaceful night and rest. I proclaimed that sweet sleep, and then I suppose I drifted off to sleep.

At some point in the night, I left this earth and found myself with you. You looked great and healthy, and peace and joy radiated from you. You had on a lavender shirt, which I'd seen you wear while you were on earth, blue jeans, and tennis shoes. And you were sitting in a large white window frame. With one leg propped on the bottom of the windowpane, and one leg hanging from it, you were just suspended in the air. I couldn't see myself, but I knew I was right there in front of you. I couldn't touch you, but I could see you and hear you as you spoke directly to me.

"Momma, you would not believe how wonderful it is here! I know you've read about it. You told me about it, but it is so much more than anyone can imagine or comprehend. I love it here, Momma. I'm fine, Momma. In fact, I'm better than fine."

Your hands were moving as you talked, and the expression on your face was priceless. There was complete peace and a penetrating joy that ruminated from you.

I don't remember saying anything to you. I'm not sure how long the vision lasted, but I knew then, and I continue to know, it was real. There you were, suspended in the glory of God. I was allowed a glimpse into your life in heaven. And it was all orchestrated by the Holy Spirit of God.

Upon waking the next morning, the vision remained alive inside me. My heart had a new and deeper measure of peace and joy. You really were okay! Reflecting on your conversation and appearance, I realized something very significant. I remembered the mole that had been on your face most of your life and the conversation we'd had about you getting it removed because you just didn't like it. And I realized son, the mole was not on your face during my vision. I knew at that moment God had given me that brief glance into the heavenlies to see the spiritual Toby. Your physical body was still in the grave at the memorial site, but your spirit was in heaven with Jesus.

Two nights later your sister, Amye, experienced the same dream/vision, and guess what—you didn't have the mole in her vision either.

Now you know I don't believe in ghosts, other than the Holy Ghost, so this was not anything like that at all. I can't explain it other than the Great Comforter somehow allowed both myself and your sister a brief visit with you in your new home. I praise Him for allowing me this onetime event. It's never happened since, and I don't expect it to happen again until I join you there in our heavenly home.

I love you forever!

Kisses from Momma

LETTER 19

Searching for Closure

If thou seekest her (wisdom) as silver, and searchest for her as for hid treasures, then shalt thou understand the fear of the Lord, and find the knowledge of God. For the Lord giveth wisdom out of His mouth cometh knowledge and understanding.
—Proverbs 2:4–6

Dear son,

Closure is something we all seek after dealing with a loss, especially a sudden, unexpected one. It's a natural reaction, and finding answers can help, but it doesn't change the results. Sometimes when death comes, we may think that if we had all the answers, we would find peace. I don't necessarily agree with that theory. Sometimes the answers only bring more confusion and grief, and the answers we've found usually lead to more questions. It becomes a vicious circle, which finds no end. I see this happening to so many people, and they find themselves wrapped up in finding answers, hoping to find some sense in the madness they've become entangled in. They are looking for validation and reason, and I believe that while we're on this earth, we will never find any valid reason why *my* child had to die a physical death.

There are not enough questions or answers to make any of us feel okay about the loss of our loved one. There's always the foundational question, "Why my child? Why my daughter? Why my son?" I can remember being out and about and seeing young men around your age and thinking to myself, *Why my son? Why not him or her?* I know that sounds terribly selfish, but it's the truth. I didn't like myself very much when I would have those thoughts, but they would just pop to the surface. Thankfully, with the help of God, I finally stopped those brutal thoughts.

One of the definitions of closure is a comforting or satisfying sense of finality: something (such as a satisfying ending) that provides such a sense. For those who have experienced the loss of a child, there is no closure. Because in our minds, there is none, nor will there ever be a reason that makes sense. We will always have a *but* or *if* in our minds of how there could have (should have) been a different and better end of the story.

Instead of closure, I sought peace—peace from the horrible nightmares, peace from the depression that wanted to overcome me, peace from the moments of losing my breath, peace from playing the scene over and over in my mind, hoping for a different outcome, only to feel powerless each time. There is no closure here on this earth, but I knew the Word of God told me there was peace available. So I sought it, and thankfully through the grace of my Lord and Savior, I found it! There have been many days and times I've had to fight to maintain that sense of peace, but God has remained faithful to me, empowering me with the ability to obtain it.

Even today, after so many years have passed, there are unanswered questions, and if I based my life upon those, I would be insane by now. I had to choose to move past the questions; I had to let them go. I choose to trust God, who does have all the answers. He doesn't always share the answers, but He always supplies peace.

I finally realized that having all the answers would never add up to an equation that would make me happy. There are no facts that will alter the devastating events which occurred on January 17, 2003. I can only accept what happened and continue to live my life here on earth. If I could, would I change it? You bet I would! At least that's my first selfish impulse, but I'm sure you wouldn't want to be yanked out of heaven and be pulled back into this sin-filled world.

So maybe I just need to leave you in a place where I will join you one day. Heaven is our destination; you just beat me there.

For now, I will choose to accept God's peace about the situation. He holds our peace in His hand, and in accepting it, I found something far better than closure. I found a treasure that gives me the ability to live each day knowing I will see you again. I can have a full life surrounded by our family and friends who also miss you, yet we choose to move forward with you forever in our hearts. One day we will all be together again, never to be separated.

That's my closure—the never-ending peace of God. That's the truth in all this: the truth of God and His peace. It is the anchor of hope that keeps my soul safe and protected. I thank Him for peace!

Kisses from Momma

LETTER 20

Forever Changed

> And it came to pass when Moses came down from mount Sinai with the two tables of testimony in Moses' hand, when he came down from the mount, that Moses wist not that the skin of his face shone while he talketh with him.
> —Exodus 34:30

My Dear Toby,

Your physical death forever changed my life and the lives of all who loved you. In the beginning, the change was not positive. But today as I sit and write this letter, I can honestly say my spiritual walk with God is much better. When you've had numerous encounters with the Lord, change comes. He held my hand during the most difficult time of my life, He heard both my loud and silent cries in the wee hours of the night, and He carried me when I didn't have the strength to carry myself. Jesus became my twenty-four-hour security detail. He never left my side, and He didn't judge me as I struggled to make sense of the devastating events that shook the core of who I was; He loved me despite myself. He became and remains my All-in-all, my Alpha and Omega, and everything in between.

Our family has always been such a great source of strength. And they helped me every single day, but it was Jesus who provided the stability I had to have in order to remain sane. When a tragic event occurs, our emotions are so raw that we sometimes don't react the way the world sees as *normal*. Our lives may seem to be out of control or irrational. Or we may withdraw and become a facade of who we want the world to see us. Either way, people may wonder if we're ever going to recover. I can honestly say, no parent ever recovers from the physical loss of their son or daughter. Life never returns to normal again. But through Jesus Christ, we can overcome the devastation and loss. It's not a quick fix nor is it easy, but it is possible.

Jesus is the only reason I am sane, and my body is healthy. Some days are more difficult than others, and each one remains a challenge if I try to handle it on my own. I'm thankful that I'm not on this journey alone; I have an awesome family, a wonderful church family, and many supporting friends, but most of all, I have King Jesus. He encourages me every single day because I ask Him to help me. In the beginning of this journey, I tried to do it on my own strength, and that was a disaster.

When you left us without warning, my heart didn't know what to do or how to feel. And I didn't know how to explain it to anyone else because there were no words to describe the way my heart felt. I wanted to feel better, I wanted to be normal, and I wanted to experience joy and laughter, yet it seemed impossible. And it was because I was trying to figure it out through my own understanding. Without the help of the Holy Spirit of God, I would still be wandering around in a fog, with a heart that consistently searched for answers that made sense when there were none to be found. My sweet son, your physical death will never make sense to me. It was only when my mind and my heart realized my only answer was the Great Comforter. When I finally submitted to Him and stopped the spirit of grief that was ruling my life, then and only then was I truly delivered and set free from the power of the enemy.

Do I still have sad days? Yes! Do I still miss you? More than I can say! Do I still experience flashbacks of those first days and weeks? Definitely! But when those times and occasions occur, I reach for the Hand that is never far from me—I cry out to the King of kings who always hears my voice, whether it's audible or in silence. And He lovingly wraps His arms around me and sings to me. Yes,

He sings to me! It is unlike anything I've ever heard—it sounds like a river, yet it brings peace to every fiber of my body, mind, and heart. My heart soars with thankfulness as I write these words. I serve a God who loves me unconditionally. There is no one like Him!

And my sweet Toby, there is no one like you! You are such a gift from God. Your face, your voice, your laughter, and even your smell will never fade from my memory. You are permanently engraved in my heart. I love you!

Kisses from Momma!

LETTER 21

Endless Tears

Thou tellest my wanderings; put thou my tears into thy bottle: are they not in thy book? When I cry unto thee then shall mine enemies turn back: this is I know, for God is for me.
—Psalm 56:8–9

Dear son,

In the first months after you left, I discovered there is no limit to the number of tears a person can produce. I would have thought that the first twenty-four hours after your departure from earth, my tear ducts would have exhausted my tears. But that was not the case! Sometimes I knew I just needed to have a good cry. It would build and build, forcing me to find somewhere private and allow the tears to flow for however long my heart required. Then there were other times, the tears fell from my eyes down my face and puddled in my heart.

Sometimes I would be driving, and right out of the blue, an episode of endless tears would surface, causing me to pull over to the side of the road on more than one occasion. If I ran into a classmate of yours, the tears were going to make an appearance. I didn't have any control over it; it just happened. And then there were the times when I would be in the shower. The sound of the water muffled the sounds of my sobbing and the water from the shower mixed in with the tears of my heart. The tears and crying did bring a temporary release. And I believe crying is good for us all if we mix in more laughter and joy than sorrow. It takes a while to balance it out, but thankfully I found that balance through the guidance of the Holy Spirit. I had to spiritually fight for the joy of the Lord, and I continue to battle for it sometimes.

I've never been a person who cried easily. So dealing with bouts of spontaneous crying or sobbing was not something I welcomed, but it happened for a season, and it still happens from time to time, but now I understand better, and I accept it. But I don't stay in that place of sorrow long—I walk out of that place of sadness. While I visit it sometimes, I don't live there anymore. And I know that you would not want that place of sadness to be a permanent residence for me.

The Word of God is filled with many scriptures on how to live an overcoming, victorious life, and that's how I fought my way out of the endless tears season of my life. Grief will overtake us if we're not careful, and it will paralyze us, taking us captive from the life Jesus died to give us. I knew the enemy wanted to steal the peace and joy that had been given to me at the time of my salvation, and I became and remain determined not to allow him to win.

To know that God stores all my tears in a bottle lets me know He genuinely cares about every single tear I shed. I think about that a lot. I've decided it must be a *large* bottle. I can almost hear your laughter and feel your hug, my handsome son!

Kisses from Momma

LETTER 22

Signs from Heaven

God also testified to it by signs, wonders and various miracles, and by gifts of the Holy Spirit distributed according to his will.
—Hebrews 2:4

Dear son,

Especially during the first year after you left earth, every single member of our family struggled in different ways for the same reason—our hearts were broken from the loss of your presence in our lives. Just as we all struggled differently, we healed differently. Our one common thread was holding on to the Lord God Jehovah. Nothing but His love and the comfort of the Holy Spirit could help us. Many people might think we are crazy, but those who have dealt with the death of a son or daughter will probably understand this letter completely. Because we chose to trust God and seek His help every single day, there were several miraculous events that took place during the first year. We knew then and we know now that only a God who loves you and wants to comfort you could have given us these signs from heaven. I don't believe God is a God of magic but a God of love and supernatural power.

One of the events we noticed shortly was finding a penny on heads. My son, we all knew you had jars and jars of pennies you'd collected. These were pennies you'd found through the years, and we knew you only saved the ones that were found on heads. I began to find an uncommon number of pennies on heads, and many times I found them in strange places. Other times I found them in common locations—sidewalks, driveways, and in yards. It's the strange places that always amazed me. Some of those locations include my shoes, the floorboard of cars, and the seats at various events. The strangest one was on a new desk. The desk arrived at my office in a sealed crate. The drawers of the desk were locked with the key taped outside the desk. When the desk was set up, and I unlocked the drawers and opened them, there was a penny on heads in the middle drawer. We all still find pennies on heads, but usually, they are in common areas now.

Another miraculous event that occurred a few months after your departure still brings tears to my eyes, yet a smile would always quickly follow. This one involves a one-dollar bill. Your nephew, Jordan, took money to a book fair held at his elementary school. After his purchase, he had a dollar left over. That night at home, he asked his mother a random question, "Are you supposed to write on money?" Your sister laughed and replied, "Your Uncle Toby used to write his name on money all the time. I told him they were going to put him in jail one day." Jordan quickly left the room and came back holding the dollar bill he had received as change that day at the book fair.

He held it out, and said, "Look at this, Momma!" Lo and behold, there in red ink was your name! Is there any reasonable explanation that a certain dollar bill made the rounds through we don't know how many hands and wound up in the hands of your nephew? Jordan missed you so much because you had been such an important part of his nine years, so this was such a treasured blessing to him, as well as to the rest of us. He continues to keep this special treasure.

We also experienced the sightings of red birds frequently, and this continues today. Maybe it's because I notice them more, but they visited me often. Sometimes I'll see five in one day, sometimes more. It always reminds me of the times when you were very young and tried many times unsuccessfully to catch red birds. Your determination never faltered, regardless of your failure to catch the red birds. I also would and still think of the verse in Luke 12:24,

> Consider the ravens: for they neither sow nor reap; which neither have storehouse nor barn: and God feedth them: how much more are ye better than the fowls?

I believe all these *unusual* events are confirmations that God cares about me and knows my every thought and memory as well as the entire family's. These red birds remind me of happy times with you and of how God provides whatever I need when I need it. There are some days I need a visit from a red bird.

There's been many more occurrences that cannot be explained in the natural or at least they can't be to me. I've learned there are no coincidences in life. I don't look for signs; they just happen, and they are always right when I need them to get through another day. Every moment, every event of our lives has a significant meaning. I cherish every special thing that God has done in my life to give me the reassurance that you are okay, and that I am okay too.

Kisses from Momma!

LETTER 23

The Results Are In

*And being full persuaded that, what He had
promised, He was able to perform.*
—Romans 4:21

My Beloved son,

This is probably the most difficult letter I've written so far. My heart literally hurts again just like it did the first days after that tragic weekend you left us. The events that led up to your physical death were now recorded on a death certificate and accompanying report from the GBI office. Although they were inconclusive, there was information that points to the cause of your death.

There have been many questions about what could have caused your death. You were twenty-six and with no known health issues, except you had recently had some acid reflux issues. We all knew you were under a lot of stress. You were working full-time, trying to maintain the academic level necessary to retain your position on the president's list at your school, and you and Brandi had recently been busy planning your fairy-tale wedding. And though you and Brandi were perfect for each other, you had only been married for a few short months, so I know there were adjustments being made in both of your lives. But we didn't think any of those or any combination of those issues were anything to be overly concerned about—maybe we were wrong.

We had received the preliminary autopsy reports earlier, and they were inconclusive. The tox screen had shown no drugs or alcohol which was a relief. The cause of death was recorded as cardiac arrest. Yet there was no recorded known cause for the cardiac arrest in a presumed healthy twenty-six-year-old male. This was all the information we had for months, and then we received news that the investigation was completed by the GBI, and their final report was available as well as the complete autopsy report.

We scheduled a family meeting, and Brandi arrived with the report. She was so distraught, so I knew the results were not good. But then again, how can any autopsy result be good? She began to share the results of the report—death by toxic inhalation. There were a lot of medical terms, but basically, the report stated the probable cause of the cardiac arrest was a result of you sniffing lighter fluid. They deduce this from the investigation by the GBI of the premises where your body was found (your and Brandi's home). This all sounded so foreign to me. I couldn't comprehend that your death occurred due to a stupid and uncalled-for choice you made.

Why son? What prompted you to make such a careless and dangerous decision? Was it to get a quick high? Was it to relieve the stresses of life? Was it just a recreational drug of choice? Why? You are dead as a result, and your family is shattered! All your hopes and dreams went with you, plus all our hopes and dreams went with you as well. Your nephew and nieces and future nieces and nephews will never get the benefit of growing up with you in their lives. What about the family you and Brandi were creating? The daughters and sons that were supposed to call you Daddy. You made a choice that was to give you what? A few seconds of escape? A brief high? And it changed everything!

That night shattered our world again. Oh, we had results, but what do we do with them now?

I must admit I stayed angry with you for a while. But I knew deep down that I could not afford to hang on to that anger. I wanted so much to talk with you and hear your side of the events of that night. But I couldn't! So I began to talk to God about all of it. In those conversations, I realized just how angry I was, and His Holy

Spirit began to counsel me. And I realized receiving the results of how you possibly could have died didn't change anything. You were still gone, and you were not coming back to this earth. The cause of death was the issue; the fact was you were dead physically. And I had to come to terms with that and realize that despite how you died, I did believe you were with Jesus. Now knowing that you possibly had left us due to a stupid useless decision, did it alter my belief that you were in heaven?

After much one-on-one time with my God, I realized, and I am and will remain fully persuaded, you are in heaven. Thank God, our stupid decisions do not change God's mind about our eternal life. Many years ago, you'd accepted Jesus Christ as your Savior, and I know it was real. I remember the dreams you had as a young boy, and I believed then, and I believe now you were saved and born again. Through the years, yes, you made some bad choices, and you paid the price for them, yet I know from the conversations we had in the weeks before your marriage, you had asked God to forgive you, and you ask for my forgiveness, which you know you already had. You told me how you continued to pray and talk to God every day and of the awesome things He'd done in your life. You had a relationship with our Father God! I'm so thankful we had those conversations, and I'm so grateful to love a God that forgives us over and over.

Because of the Blood of Jesus Christ, you now abide in heaven, and I too, despite all my wrong choices, will join you in eternity.

I am no longer angry. God promised me many years ago, all my children would be saved, and my children's children and on, and He is keeping His promise to me. I believe the second your physical heart stopped breathing, Jesus was right there beside you, holding out His hand and leading you right to the gates of heaven where He entered with you. You were never alone, not for one second. I am fully persuaded that everything God said He would do, He did and continues to do. I thank Him for saving *you*! I thank Him for saving me and my family. I thank *Him* for being my God!

I love you, son, and you are forgiven. I ask you to forgive me.

Kisses from Momma

LETTER 24

Overcoming Regrets and Guilt

And I heard a loud voice saying in heaven, Now is come salvation, and strength, and the kingdom of our God, and the power of his Christ; for the accuser of our brethren is cast down, which accused them before our God day and night.
—Revelation 12:10

Dear Toby,

I'm looking forward to the day our accuser is cast down! The end is coming for Satan! God is the *victor*, and therefore so am I, as His child. There were times I didn't feel too victorious, but His Word still says I am!

There have been many times the accuser had attacked my thoughts, as well as the rest of your family. He uses two major thought patterns—regret and guilt.

Guilt comes in like a vicious attack dog, charging every part of your mind with its angry teeth, ripping every shred of peace you are hanging on to throughout the days. The spirit of guilt is not pretty; it has no respect, no manners, and no remorse.

Regret is a constant reminder by the enemy of the what-ifs and the whys. And they continually pound upon your thoughts and emotions until you feel helpless and hopeless. They both come in quickly and take you as hostages. Every family member finds themselves in some type of bondage. The enemy will try to convince you he, and only he, holds the keys. But Satan is a liar; there is no truth in him (John 8:44–45).

Guilt has the power to take you back to every decision you've ever made as a parent and causes you to question it. Guilt never points to the future but always to the past. Regret reminds you of the what-ifs. What if you had said this or done that? It's a vicious cycle that sweeps in and takes control of your life. *If* we allow it to take control.

I thank God for placing people in our lives that had not only experienced what we were going through, but who, through the power of Christ, had not only survived it but had become overcomers. They shared their stories and the Word of God with us and helped us see the attacks we were experiencing did not have to take control over our lives. We had a choice; we had power over every single lie and every thought of guilt and regret because of Who we belonged to!

Thank God for His Holy Spirit! Without His balance, His counsel, and His unconditional love, mercy, and grace, we could have been swallowed into the unending gulf of guilt.

Life doesn't give us a do-over for our past, but it does allow us to choose to follow our Life-giver, Jesus Christ. We have the free choice to listen to the lies of the enemy or to hear and live by the Truth of our Savior, Jesus Christ. He is the Truth, He is the Way, and He will guide us into all Truth.

Did we or do we always get it right as parents? Definitely not! But our decisions were based on our love for each of you as our children. We never purposely decided to harm any of you, and we never would. We know we made some wrong choices, but those are now looking through twenty-twenty hindsight. Most parents do the best we can with the information we currently have, and that sometimes unfortunately involves not having all the information or having the correct information. However, we love you all unconditionally, and we put each of you in a position to know and have a relationship with Jesus Christ. Those decisions were the best we could offer, and any others we got right were just icing on the cake.

Guilt and regret are powerful spirits, yet neither changes anything, except for causing further damage to an individual. Once we recognized what was happening, we took authority over those thought patterns and took control away from the enemy.

Instead of regret and guilt, we now chose to celebrate the good memories and the shared laughter throughout the years, and yes, we talk about the hard times too. But we don't live in regret, and we don't allow guilt to be a part of our conversations anymore. We have so much to be thankful for in our lives, and even though you aren't physically present, you are forever present in our hearts and thoughts.

We chose to evict guilt and regret. Sometimes in the distance, I hear their familiar knock, but I refuse to open the door. I tell others, "Regret and guilt are powerless unless we give them power." It's a choice.

I love you, my son, and miss you every single day!

Kisses from Momma

LETTER 25

The Mind versus the Heart

> *Thou wilt keep him in perfect peace, whose mind is stayed on thee: because he trusteth in thee.*
> —Isaiah 26:3

My dear son,

The months following your departure were strange times. As time passed, some things became more bearable. But the intense longing to see you did not lessen at all. In fact, each passing day seemed to be more difficult than the previous.

My mind played horrible tricks on me at times. Sometimes I would be so sure I heard you calling out to me, "Momma, Momma." Wherever I was, I would search for you, knowing it would of no avail.

There were times I was certain I'd seen you in a passing car. I must admit, many of those times, I would make a U-turn and follow the car, knowing in my mind how ridiculous my actions were, yet my heart urged me to follow.

And then there were the times I'd see your face in a crowd. My heartbeat would increase and for a few seconds, hope would elevate inside of me, and I would walk closer and even stare as my heart persisted to believe it was you. And then that hope would deflate as I would realize I was looking at a stranger.

Looking back, I think my heart wanted to see you, needed to see you so badly, and allowed my mind to see what my heart wanted to see. My mind knew the truth, but my heart still could not fully accept the reality of what my life had become. After the death of a child, there can be a great distance of miles from your heart to your mind. Your mind usually knows the truth, but your heart wants to deny it. Repeatedly, I would find my mind having to convince my heart that I didn't really see or hear you. I desperately wanted my heart to win at least one time, but it never did.

Until the time comes for my departure to heaven, I have photos of you and twenty-six years of memories of you stored in my mind and heart. And one sweet day, we will be joined together in our forever home, heaven. Heaven will be a great homecoming, with the greatest being looking face to face at my Lord and finally being able to worship Him and thank Him for being my Lord. And I will also be forever joined by you and other loved ones. I'm sure your infectious laughter will ring through the heavenly realms at that time. Oh, what a glorious time that will be. Looking every day for the return of our Lord Jesus Christ!

Kisses from Momma

LETTER 26

Learning to Forgive

And forgive us our debts, as we forgive our debtors.
—Matthew 6:12

Dear sweet Toby,

Forgiveness—such a powerful and freeing word but one that sometimes seems so difficult to daily walk in.

After receiving the certified report of your physical death, I was angry with you for a little while. I didn't want to be, and I knew my anger wasn't going to change the events at the time of your death, yet there I dwelt.

The Word of God is very clear on unforgiveness, and I knew it was not anything I needed to entertain in my life, but it took some time and a lot of faith to get myself past the feelings I had. I wasn't angry at you as much as I was angry at the choice you'd made that January night. Your choice had cost you your life, and it had cost your family and friends *you*!

I've never been a person who can stay mad or angry with anyone very long, especially one of my children. I don't hold grudges, and I don't usually take offense easily. But my heart hurt because I blamed you for your own early death. I still loved you with all my heart, but I was so caught up in the *what-ifs* that I could only feel the anger, and

I pointed it toward you and anyone who happened to be involved in the events that had taken place.

The blame game is as old as Adam and Eve. Genesis 3:11–23 is where the blame game began, and it continues.

> And he said, who told thee that thou wast naked? Hast thou eaten of the tree, whereof I commanded thee that thou shouldest not eat? And the man said, the woman whom thou gavest to be with me, she gave me of the tree, and I did eat.

Unforgiveness brings along a trunk load of emotions. Anger, guilt, regret, and so many other emotions begin to camp out in our minds. And when you mix grief and sorrow to the mix, it's not a good frame of mind for anyone. Neither Christians nor non-Christians are exempt from any of these negative stealers.

Thankfully, in the past, I'd experienced some awesome teaching on forgiveness, so I knew I had to make a choice to first ask God to forgive me for entertaining all the thoughts I'd given permission to camp out in my mind. Then I had to forgive you, my beautiful sweet son. The anger, regret, and guilt began to subside as I began to forgive you. I've had many one-sided talks with you during those weeks as I went through the process of forgiveness. And it is a process. It doesn't happen overnight, but it began the minute I asked God to help me forgive.

Then the process of forgiving everyone else I'd somehow blamed or had negative thoughts toward began. I asked our Heavenly Father to help me sort out anyone I'd blamed or resented by their innocent connection to you or the events of your physical death. I was never vocal about my unforgiveness to anyone, but I'd had the thoughts regardless, so I had to repent of my thoughts, and I thank God; He forgave me.

I'm so thankful that I walk in His forgiveness every single day. Christ forgave and forgives me every single day for my wrong choices. Some wrong choices cost more than others. Yours cost you, and those who love you, the ultimate price. Yet Christ forgave you just as He forgives me and everyone else who asks Him to forgive them. He wipes the slate clean every single time. His mercies are new every morning, regardless of what my situation may be. Thank God, His grace is not determined or measured by my choices or circumstances.

During this time, God brought to my remembrance what a forgiving child you were. You never held grudges, and the words, "I'm sorry," came easily for you. I know you left earth without any unforgiveness in your heart. That's just the kind of person you were on this earth. I am learning from your example.

Thank you, son, for forgiving me for the times I failed you as a mother. We both know that any failures on my part were not a love problem because I love you with all my heart. Parents learn through experience, and sometimes those most precious to us suffer from our ignorance. But in the end, I know in my heart that you knew the depth and width of the love I had, and your whole family had for you.

Kisses from your forgiven Momma

LETTER 27

The First of Many

*To every*thing there is *a season, and a time
to every purpose under the heaven:
A time to be born, and a time to die; a time to plant,
and a time to pluck up* that which is *planted;
A time to kill, and a time to heal; a time to
break down, and a time to build up;
A time to weep, and a time to laugh; a time
to mourn, and a time to dance;
A time to cast away stones, and a time to gather stones together;
a time to embrace, and a time to refrain from embracing;
A time to get, and a time to lose; a time to
keep, and a time to cast away;
A time to rend, and a time to sew; a time to
keep silence, and a time to speak;
A time to love, and a time to hate; a time of war, and a time of peace.*
—Ecclesiastes 3:1–8

Dear Toby,

One of the most common phrases people say when speaking to someone who has lost a loved one is, "Time will heal. Time will help. In time this, and in time that." That's not true. Time is not the all-time answer, nor does it bring any comfort at all to the one who is going through the worst possible situation. Whatever has happened in the past or whatever is going to happen in the future, we are always dealing with loss in the present. Losing a child to physical death is not made better in time. We deal with it every single day, sometimes every single hour. And there are certain times of the year such as holidays, vacations, birthdays, and family events that regardless of how much time has passed since you left us, the loss is felt one hundred percent, the first time, the fifth time, the tenth time, and forever on this side of heaven.

There's the first vacation we took as a family without you. I debated on doing a family vacation the first year. Only six long months had passed. We as a family finally decided to take one but not to our usual destination. That would just be too hard we decided. So we chose a new destination, and off we went. It went okay. But it was not the same, nor has it ever been. Time does not heal all wounds.

Then there are birthdays, family events like weddings, births, and even family deaths; you are always missing. It doesn't get better; we've just learned to adjust but never assume that there's not a *big* void in our hearts and conversations. It's hard to explain, son, but sometimes I just miss your comical answers or your serious input. Stories about you surface often during our family get-togethers. Some of them told so many times, they must be frayed around the conversation lines. But we continue to reminisce and share the stories, usually flooded with laughter.

Christmas is especially difficult because you loved the season so much. I miss shopping for you. I still to this day see things I know you would love. Certain colors would come to my attention, and I think about how handsome you would look. Time does not heal all wounds.

Mother's Day is not easy either. You know how much I love your sister and brothers, and they always try to make it special for me, but you are always missed so much! Time does not make it better.

You are missed every single day, but there are some days there's just a bigger void. The first year was the toughest to get through, but the many which have followed are not much easier. But always know, Toby, each year as we celebrate various events in our lives, you are present with us inside our thoughts, our conversations, and our hearts. You are forever missed and loved!

    I have learned that although time does not heal all wounds, there is *One* who does, and His name is Jesus Christ. During the first year, I could barely breathe at times, though I tried to cover how helpless I truly felt from my family and my friends. I couldn't hide it from God, and He faithfully gave me the strength to overcome my weaknesses. And even now, almost twenty years later, I continue to lose my breath sometimes. But our God brings joy into my life through your daddy, your siblings, your nieces and nephews, your family, and your friends. He reminds me of how truly blessed I am. I have the promise of eternal life with Christ Jesus. I have the promise of heaven in my future, and there, I will celebrate eternally with you as we will both be in the presence of our Savior.

Kisses from Momma

LETTER 28

Limited Visitation

Finally, brethren, whatsoever things are true, whatsoever things are honest, whatsoever things are just, whatsoever things are pure, whatsoever things are lovely, whatsoever things are of good report; if there be any virtue, and if there be any praise, think on these things. Those things, which ye have both learned, and received, and heard, and seen in me, do: and the God of peace shall be with you.
—Philippians 4:8–9

Dear sweet son,

My heart longs to see you, to hug you. I tell myself, if I could just have one day with you, yet I know that would never be enough. Time keeps racing by, as year after year comes and goes, and I know in my spirit that the rapture draws nearer each day. There will be a great reunion soon my son.

    In the meantime, my mind sometimes slips back to the night of January 18, 2002. From the phone call and throughout the next months, my mind sometimes seems to get stuck in a time capsule and I can't escape. I feel the disbelief, I experience the false hope that it's all a dream, the sadness creeps in, and sometimes the tears come. It's like a replay of all the events of those terrible months of not knowing what happened, not understanding how it happened, and having endless questions that have no answers. The result is nothing changes, regardless of the length of time that has passed. The bottom line remains the same—you are not with us!

There are times when what I call *trigger points* will create a return voyage into the most painful time of my life. Sometimes when I see a classmate or friend of yours at the recreation park watching their kids play ball. I do the *what-if* scenario and wonder who your children would look like. Would they have your quick wit and mind? I think about you and your beautiful wife and the anniversaries you would have celebrated by now. I think about the pride you would have for your brothers and sister. These trigger points and return voyages are dangerous and unhealthy for me. So I must choose to stop the visit going on in my mind. I've learned it's okay to visit for a very limited time, and then I must evict myself from the memories. Not all memories are meant for long-term residence. Memories should bring peace and joy, not heartache. I chose the memories I want to visit and how long I want to stay.

My son, I've had to accept the truth that I'll never be a grandmommy to your children, nor will I celebrate with you physically by my side again, nor can I change the past. I don't like any of it, and I never will, but I can now live without all the grief, pain, and sorrow consuming me. And it's only because *He* lives. The Holy Spirit of God inside me has taught me so much about myself. I've learned who I am and who I belong to, and that is how I can do exactly what Philippians 4:8–9 tells us to do.

Instead of abiding in a state of loss and grief, I make the choice every day to think about those things that are pure, honest, and just, things that are pure and lovely and good report. My future is bright and full of the promises of God. My days must consist of these thoughts. I truly want my testimony to be a praise to our Lord Jesus. I find much comfort in verse 9—God's peace shall be with you (me). And I can certainly verify that He is with me through it all.

Kisses from Momma

LETTER 29

Your Family

But as for me and my house, we will serve the LORD."
—Joshua 24:15

Dear Toby,

I've always known I wanted to be a mother, even as a child. My parents (your MaMa and PaPa) were great parents. I was blessed to have grandparents and lots of aunts and uncles, and cousins. Growing up was a fun time full of large family get-togethers who loved and showed love, so family was instilled in me. There was never a question of if I would have children, just when.

Through the years, I was blessed with four beautiful, smart, full-of-personality children. Three I physically birthed, and one I birthed in my heart. Being a blended family may have brought its challenges through the years, but one thing for sure is our love for God and each other was always greater than the challenges.

Though your wonderful daddy didn't physically have anything to do with your birth, he was and is your daddy in every way. You fell in love with him almost instantly, and the feeling was mutual. Your daddy always wanted to make things better for you and wanted to be sure you knew how much he loved you. Your big sister Amye has loved you as long as I've loved you, and she has always been so protective of you, but she was also your partner in crime sometimes. Your older brother Cahn, who I birthed in my heart, was also your protector and always wanted to be there for you. I know you were a pain to both him and Amye as they began to get older, and there you were, always wanting to tag along. They tolerated it most of the time. And then there was Josh, the baby of the family. You were so proud to be a big brother, and you were so good at it. While Amye and Cahn always found something more important to do when it was time to feed him or change his diaper, there you would be, willing even excited to do it. There was no task you wouldn't undertake for Josh. And he looked up to you as his big brother, and he loves you *big*. They all love you! We all love you.

Your physical death impacted each of us in our own way, and as a family unit as well. There's been days we didn't know what to say or what to do. Times of tears, more times of laughter, and times of love. In my letters to you, I've shared my heart. Each of them has their own heart stories of dealing with the loss of you, but it's their stories to tell. I know they miss you more than words can explain, and their hearts, even now, are still so tender toward you, their brother.

When we became a blended family, as parents, we made a decision to serve the Lord as a family. And the rule was we loved God, we went to church, and we lived our lives as an example of Jesus the best we could. We didn't and still don't always make the mark, but our hearts are set on Him. And we've never regretted that decision. It literally changed and saved our lives.

Our family misses you, sweet Toby, so much! Yet we continue to move forward, loving each other, depending on each other, and looking forward to everything God has planned for our lives. And somehow I know you know!

Some nights, when I look into the sky and see the marvelous works of our God, I will see a star sparkle just a little brighter, and I just know you're playing with the stars. I can almost see a wink in your eyes, as you look at the Father, and He winks back. I know that I know you're in the presence of the Most High God, and for that we, your family, are grateful.

We will see you on the other side of the stars!

Kisses from Momma

LETTER 30

Kisses from Momma

Dearest son,

During the time you've been gone, I've had so many conversations with God about my struggles as well as my victories. I give credit to all my victories to my Lord, who holds my hand every day. Without Him, the struggles would win.

On so many of those conversations I've ended with this request of God:

"Dear Lord, please give my sweet boy Toby a kiss for me, and tell him it's from his momma." Thus, the title of this little book of heart letters to you. And you know what, my son? I know He does it because He loves me, and He loves you. One day soon, I will be able to kiss you myself, right after I kiss Jesus, the One who sustains me every second of every day. But until then,

Lord, please do it again. Kiss my sweet boy Toby and tell him it's from his momma.

With all my love and kisses from Momma!

EPILOGUE

Kisses from Momma is a collection of letters I've written to my son Toby who now resides in heaven. I began writing them shortly after his unexpected death. And I've continued through the years. I don't write to him now as often as I did in the beginning, yet there are still times I find myself drawn to put my thoughts on paper and have a conversation with him.

It never occurred to share them until one day I was sharing just one letter with another mother who'd lost an adult child, and she suggested I share them to let mothers know they were not the only ones having some of these thoughts and emotions. A few years later, the Holy Spirit of God confirmed the idea. And I began the journey, and it's been long and difficult to share the deepest wounds of my heart. I thank God for His continued encouragement and help as well as for my family and friends.

There are some parts I didn't want to share, but I know there's someone reading who needs to know even the hardest of truths.

My prayer is that those who are hurting from the loss of a child, regardless of age, can see there's hope in the midst of all the confusion, heartache, and helplessness. I encourage you, if you don't already know Jesus Christ, to begin to search for Him. He's easy to find, and He's waiting on you to discover Him. If you are already a Christian, then I encourage you to develop a deeper relationship with Him than you've ever experienced. You can be honest with Him, you can share every thought with Him, and He won't ever judge you. He will only love you! He will restore your joy, your sanity, and your peace.

I also encourage you to write your thoughts down. Buy a journal or notebook and jot down your feelings. Have a conversation on paper with your beloved child.

To all those who belong to the exclusive club of being a parent who has lost a child to death, I say blessings to each of you. Even though I don't know you or your name, I pray for you each day. The One True God I pray to knows who you are and knows you by name. We never asked to belong to this club, and I would like to be expounded from it, but it's a lifetime membership, and there's no escape from it. But the Captain of the host, the Most High Jesus Christ, shares His membership into the kingdom of heaven with me, and that membership is what gets me through.

Our family continues to miss Toby every day, but we are thriving and increasing. My husband and I have five grandchildren, with a set of twins due in a few months, and two great-grandkids. Our children continue to share stories with them of their uncle Toby. Much has transpired in the years our sweet Toby had been in heaven, but the love in our hearts has remained as steadfast and strong as ever, and that will continue.

ABOUT THE AUTHOR

Shirley is a Christian wife, mother, grandmother, and great-grandmother. Other than writing and spending time with her family, she spends her time as an associate pastor/teacher and associate real estate broker. She writes from her heart and real-life experiences. As a teacher at a local church, she and her husband/pastor research and write Bible lessons and study guides that are taught regularly. The message in her book, *Kisses from Momma*, is honest even when sharing the most painful experiences she's walked through. The focus of her book is to give readers hope that they too cannot only survive but also overcome every parent's worst nightmare.

Printed in the USA
CPSIA information can be obtained
at www.ICGtesting.com
LVHW090832140224
771720LV00003B/432